Superstars of Wrestling

SASHA BANKS

BY BENJAMIN PROUDFIT

Gareth Stevens
PUBLISHING

Please visit our website, www.garethstevens.com. For a free color catalog of all our high-quality books, call toll free 1-800-542-2595 or fax 1-877-542-2596.

Library of Congress Cataloging-in-Publication Data

Names: Proudfit, Benjamin, author.
Title: Sasha Banks / Benjamin Proudfit.
Description: New York : Gareth Stevens Publishing, 2022. | Series: Superstars of wrestling | Includes index.
Identifiers: LCCN 2020032255 (print) | LCCN 2020032256 (ebook) | ISBN 9781538265994 (library binding) | ISBN 9781538265970 (paperback) | ISBN 9781538265987 (set) | ISBN 9781538266007 (ebook)
Subjects: LCSH: Banks, Sasha, 1992---Juvenile literature. | World Wrestling Entertainment, Inc.--Biography--Juvenile literature. | Women wrestlers--United States--Biography--Juvenile literature.
Classification: LCC GV1196.B36 P76 2022 (print) | LCC GV1196.B36 (ebook) | DDC 796.812092 [B]--dc23
LC record available at https://lccn.loc.gov/2020032255
LC ebook record available at https://lccn.loc.gov/2020032256

First Edition

Published in 2022 by
Gareth Stevens Publishing
29 E. 21st Street
New York, NY 10010

Copyright © 2022 Gareth Stevens Publishing

Designer: Michael Flynn
Editor: Kristen Nelson

Photo credits: Cover, pp. 1, 25 Lukas Schulze/Bongarts/Getty Images; p. 5 Jon Kopaloff/Stringer/Getty Images; p. 7 Steven Paston/PA Images/Getty Images; p. 9 https://commons.wikimedia.org/wiki/Category:Mercedes_Kaestner-Varnado#/media/File:Sasha_Banks_WrestleMania_Axxess_2015.jpg; p. 11 https://commons.wikimedia.org/wiki/File:WWE_NXT_2015-03-28_00-17-14_ILCE-6000_3932_DxO_(16744451474).jpg; pp. 13, 19 Sylvain Lefevre/Getty Images; p. 15 https://commons.wikimedia.org/wiki/File:WWE_Raw_2016-04-04_19-40-26_ILCE-6000_2497_DxO_(28352231546).jpg; p. 17 https://commons.wikimedia.org/wiki/Category:Mercedes_Kaestner-Varnado#/media/File:WWE_Raw_2016-04-04_19-40-26_ILCE-6000_2497_DxO_; p. 21 Dominik Bindl/Getty Images; p. 23 Bennett Raglin/Getty Images; p. 27 Etsuo Hara/Getty Images; p. 29 Newspix/Getty Images.

All rights reserved. No part of this book may be reproduced in any form without permission in writing from the publisher, except by a reviewer.

Printed in the United States of America

CPSIA compliance information: Batch #CSGS22: For further information contact Gareth Stevens, New York, New York at 1-800-542-2595.

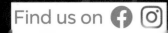

CONTENTS

A Star Is Born	4
Big Beginnings	8
WrestleMania Moment	14
Women's Firsts	16
Teaming Up	24
Reaching Higher	28
The Best of Sasha Banks	30
For More Information	31
Glossary	32
Index	32

A STAR IS BORN

Sasha Banks is "The Boss" of World Wrestling Entertainment (WWE). But, before she became a star in the women's **division**, she was Mercedes Kaestner-Varnado, born January 26, 1992, in California. Her family moved around a lot when she was growing up.

IN THE RING

Sasha calls Boston, Massachusetts, her hometown even though she wasn't born there.

Sasha started going to school online-only when she was 13. She wanted to help her mom take care of her brother, Joshua. By then, she already wanted to be a **professional** wrestler. She started training in the ring as a teenager.

IN THE RING

Sasha's family moved around a lot partly to find better schools and doctors to help with her brother's health problems.

BIG BEGINNINGS

Sasha tried out for WWE in 2012. She signed a contract to wrestle in NXT, and soon started using the in-ring name Sasha Banks. Her first **match** was in December 2012 against Paige.

IN THE RING

Sasha used her real name, Mercedes, as her first in-ring name.

By 2014, Sasha, Becky Lynch, Charlotte Flair, and Bayley were calling themselves the Four Horsewomen. They led the NXT women's division. Then, in February 2015, Sasha beat them all to win the NXT Women's Championship at NXT TakeOver: Rival!

IN THE RING

Sasha, along with Charlotte and Becky, was brought up to one of WWE's main TV shows, *Raw*, in July 2015.

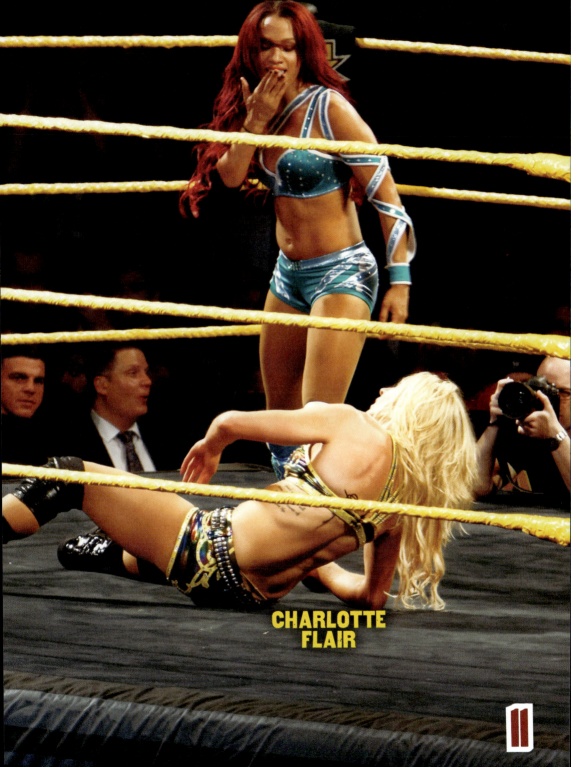

Sasha was still champion when she **debuted** on *Raw*. In August 2015, she faced Bayley at NXT: Brooklyn in what was later called the best women's wrestling match of all time! Sasha lost the title to Bayley, but it was an important moment in her **career**.

BAYLEY

IN THE RING

Sasha and Bayley have both feuded, or fought, and worked together for much of their time in NXT and WWE.

13

WRESTLEMANIA MOMENT

Sasha's career has been marked by matches featuring the other Four Horsewomen. At WrestleMania 32 in April 2016, she faced Becky Lynch and Charlotte Flair for the new WWE Women's Championship. Sasha's cousin, rapper Snoop Dogg, walked her to the ring!

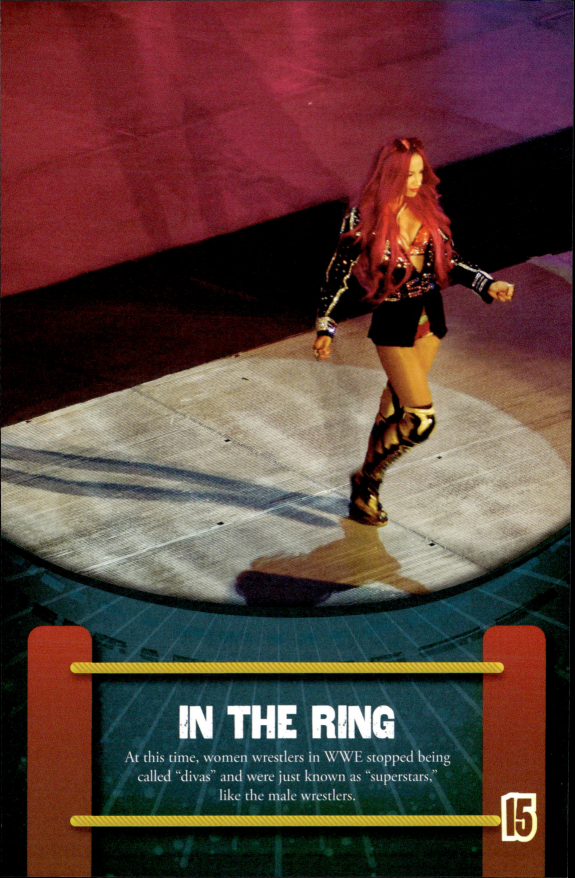

IN THE RING

At this time, women wrestlers in WWE stopped being called "divas" and were just known as "superstars," like the male wrestlers.

15

WOMEN'S FIRSTS

Since 2016, Sasha has taken part in many firsts for women in the WWE. On October 4, 2016, Sasha and Charlotte Flair became the first women to be the main event of *Raw* in 12 years. Sasha won her first WWE championship that night!

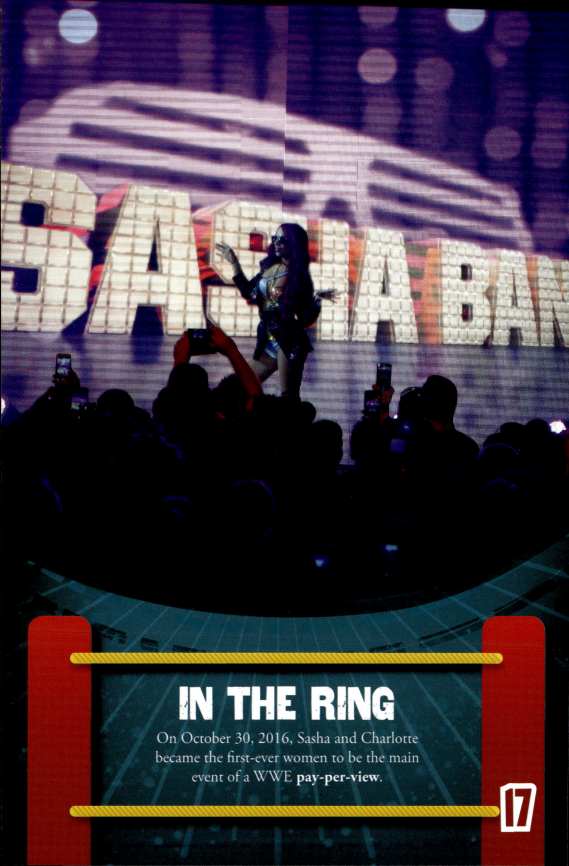

IN THE RING

On October 30, 2016, Sasha and Charlotte became the first-ever women to be the main event of a WWE **pay-per-view**.

17

On the road to WrestleMania 33, Sasha won and lost the Raw Women's Championship. She faced Charlotte Flair, Nia Jax, and Bayley in a Fatal 4-Way at WrestleMania in April 2017. Sasha lost after hitting the corner of the ring face-first.

IN THE RING

Sasha won the Raw Women's Championship from Alexa Bliss at SummerSlam 2017.

Sasha faced Alexa Bliss again in December 2017 in Abu Dhabi, United Arab Emirates. They were the first WWE women's match in the Middle East. They wore special **gear** that only showed their heads and hands to follow local laws.

IN THE RING

Women in the crowd in Abu Dhabi shouted during the match: "This is hope!"

In January 2018, the first Women's Royal Rumble match heavily featured Sasha. She was the first to enter the ring and the woman to last the longest in the match. A few weeks later, Sasha was part of the first-ever women's elimination chamber match!

IN THE RING

Sasha wrote about her excitement for the first women's Royal Rumble on ESPN.com: "The thought of participating in a Royal Rumble rates a 100 on a scale of 1 to 10 for me."

TEAMING UP

In mid 2018, Sasha and Bayley began to work together as a tag team called the Boss 'n' Hug Connection. They entered the elimination chamber again in February 2019, working together against six other tag teams.

BAYLEY

IN THE RING

The Boss 'n' Hug Connection won the match, becoming the first WWE Women's Tag Team Champions!

Sasha and Bayley **defended** the tag team titles at WrestleMania 35. They lost them to Billie Kay and Peyton Royce. Sasha took time off following the disappointing loss. She returned in August 2019 as a heel!

IN THE RING

"Heel" is a professional wrestling word for a bad guy. Sasha has been both a heel and face, or good guy, during her career with WWE.

REACHING HIGHER

Sasha continues to be one of the top stars of the women's division in WWE. At WrestleMania 36 in April 2020, she fought for the SmackDown Women's Championship. By June she and Bayley again became tag team champs! What's next for Sasha?

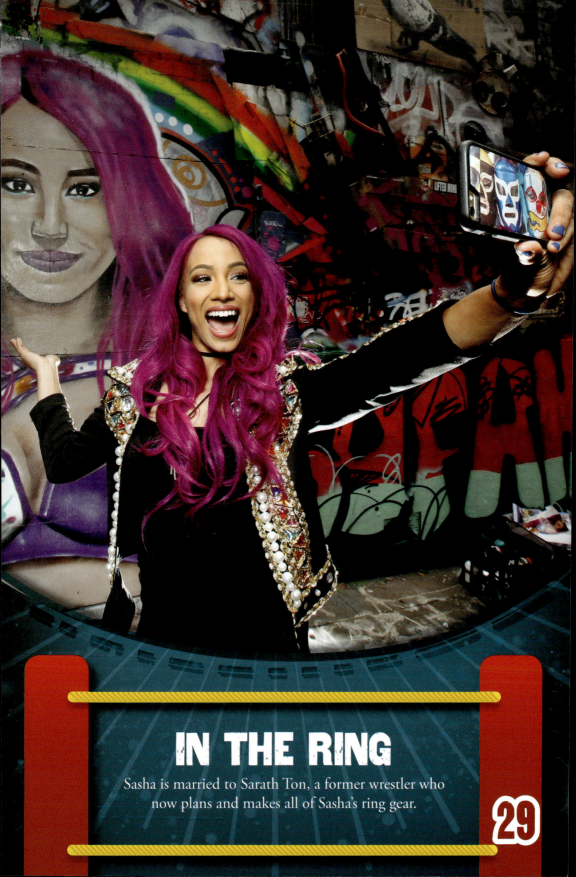

IN THE RING

Sasha is married to Sarath Ton, a former wrestler who now plans and makes all of Sasha's ring gear.

29

THE BEST OF SASHA BANKS

SIGNATURE MOVES
hurricanrana, camel clutch, suicide dive

FINISHERS
bank statement

ACCOMPLISHMENTS
NXT Women's Champion
WWE Women's Tag Team
Champion
Raw Women's Champion

MATCHES TO WATCH
NXT TakeOver: Brooklyn vs. Bayley; NXT TakeOver: Respect vs. Bayley; WrestleMania 32 vs. Charlotte Flair vs. Becky Lynch

FOR MORE INFORMATION

BOOKS

Black, Jake. *WWE Ultimate Superstar Guide.* New York, NY: DK | Penguin Random House, 2018.

Pantaleo, Steve. *How to Win in the Ring.* New York, NY: DK Publishing, 2019.

WEBSITES

Sasha Banks | WWE
www.wwe.com/superstars/sasha-banks
Keep up with Sasha Banks on her official WWE website.

WWE Profile: Sasha Banks
www.espn.com/wwe/story/_/id/17173311/wwe-profile-page-sasha-banks
Find out the latest about Sasha Banks on her ESPN profile.

Publisher's note to educators and parents: Our editors have carefully reviewed these websites to ensure that they are suitable for students. Many websites change frequently, however, and we cannot guarantee that a site's future contents will continue to meet our high standards of quality and educational value. Be advised that students should be closely supervised whenever they access the internet.

GLOSSARY

career: a job someone does for a long time

debut: to make a first appearance

defend: to fight to keep

division: a group of teams or people that compete against each other

gear: special clothes worn in professional wrestling

match: a contest between two or more people

pay-per-view: a television service by which people pay a fee to watch a particular show or event

professional: earning money from an activity that many people do for fun

INDEX

Bayley 10, 12, 13, 18, 19, 24, 25, 26, 28

Bliss, Alexa 18, 19, 20

Boss 'n' Hug Connection 24, 25

Boston, Massachusetts 5

Flair, Charlotte 10, 11, 14, 16, 17, 18

Four Horsewomen 10, 14

heel 26

Kay, Billie 26, 27

Lynch, Becky 10, 14

NXT 8, 10, 12, 13

Paige 8

pay-per-view 17

Raw 10, 12, 16, 18

Royal Rumble 22

Royce, Peyton 26, 27

Snoop Dogg 14

Ton, Sarath 29

United Arab Emirates 20

WrestleMania 14, 18, 26, 28